EASY MAC AND CHEESE COOKBOOK

THE EFFORTLESS CHEF SERIES

VOL. #XX

By
Chef Maggie Chow
Copyright © 2015 by Saxonberg
Associates

Published by
BookSumo, a division of Saxonberg
Associates
http://www.booksumo.com/

A GIFT FROM ME TO YOU...

Send the Book!

I know you like easy cooking. But what about Japanese Sushi?

Join my private reader's club and get a copy of ***Infinite Sushi: A Complete Set of Sushi and Japanese Recipes*** by fellow BookSumo author Hashimoto Kazuma for FREE!

<u>Send the Book!</u>

Enjoy some of the best sushi available!

You will also receive updates about all my new books when they are free. So please show your support.

Also don't forget to like and subscribe on the social networks. I love meeting my readers. Links to all my profiles are below so please click and connect :)

<u>Facebook</u>

<u>Twitter</u>

ABOUT THE AUTHOR.

Maggie Chow is the author and creator of your favorite *Easy Cookbooks* and *The Effortless Chef Series*. Maggie is a lover of all things related to food. Maggie loves nothing more than finding new recipes, trying them out, and then making them her own, by adding or removing ingredients, tweaking cooking times, and anything to make the recipe not only taste better, but be easier to cook!

For a complete listing of all my books please see my author page at:

http://amazon.com/author/maggiechow

INTRODUCTION

Welcome to *The Effortless Chef Series*! Thank you for taking the time to download the *Easy Mac and Cheese Cookbook*. Come take a journey with me into the delights of easy cooking. The point of this cookbook and all my cookbooks is to exemplify the effortless nature of cooking simply.

In this book we focus on Mac and Cheese. You will find that even though the recipes are simple, the taste of the dishes is quite amazing.

So will you join me in an adventure of simple cooking? If the answer is yes (and I hope it is) please consult the table of contents to find the dishes you are most interested in. Once you are ready jump right in and start cooking.

— Chef Maggie Chow

TABLE OF CONTENTS

NOTICE TO PRINT READERS:

Hey, because you purchased the print version of this book you are entitled to its original digital version for free by Amazon.

So when you have the time, please review your purchases, and download the Kindle version of this book.

You might enjoy consuming this book more in its original digital format.

;)

But, in any case, take care and enjoy reading in whatever format you choose!

Any Issues? Contact Me

If you find that something important to you is missing from this book please contact me at maggie@booksumo.com.

I will try my best to re-publish a revised copy taking your feedback into consideration and let you know when the book has been revised with you in mind.

:)

— Chef Maggie Chow

LEGAL NOTES

Chapter 1: Easy Mac and Cheese Recipes

The Quickest Mac 'n' Cheese

Ingredients

- 1 cup macaroni
- 1/2 cup process cheese sauce
- 2 frankfurters, sliced
- 1 tsp grated Parmesan cheese
- 1 pinch dried oregano
- 4 buttery round crackers, crushed

Directions

- Set your oven at 350 degrees F.
- Cook pasta in salty boiling water for about 10 minutes until tender before draining it.
- Heat up cheese sauce in microwave for about 1 minute before baking the mixture of

cooked pasta, oregano, cheese sauce, parmesan and sliced frankfurters for about 10 minutes.

- Serve.

Serving: 4

Timing Information:

Preparation	Cooking	Total Time
2 mins	13 mins	15 mins

Nutritional Information:

Calories	284 kcal
Carbohydrates	25.9 g
Cholesterol	36 mg
Fat	14.9 g
Fiber	1.5 g
Protein	10.8 g
Sodium	829 mg

* Percent Daily Values are based on a 2,000 calorie diet.
Nutrition

MEXICAN MAC AND CHEESE

Ingredients

- 1 pound ground round
- 1 tsp minced garlic
- 1 (16 ounce) jar chunky salsa
- 2 cups water
- 1 (7 ounce) package elbow macaroni
- 12 ounces processed cheese food (such as Velveeta®), cut into 1 1/2-inch chunks

Directions

- Cook beef and garlic in a large skillet over high heat for about seven minutes or until brown.
- Bring the mixture of salsa and water to boil before adding macaroni and cooking it for another 10 minutes or until tender.

- Add cheese into the skillet before serving.

Serving: 4

Timing Information:

Preparation	Cooking	Total Time
10 mins	15 mins	25 mins

Nutritional Information:

Calories	604 kcal
Carbohydrates	51.3 g
Cholesterol	92 mg
Fat	27.5 g
Fiber	3.4 g
Protein	38 g
Sodium	1518 mg

* Percent Daily Values are based on a 2,000 calorie diet.
☐

MAC AND CHEESE PIZZA

Ingredients

- 1 (12 inch) pre-baked pizza crust
- 3/4 cup cavatappi (corkscrew macaroni)
- 2/3 (16 ounce) jar cheese sauce (such as Ragu® Double Cheddar), divided, or as needed
- 1 tbsps butter
- salt and ground black pepper to taste
- 1/2 cup shredded Cheddar cheese

Directions

- Set your oven at 450 degrees F and put pizza crust on a baking dish.
- Cook cavatappi in boiling salty water for about 11 minutes before draining and putting it back in the pot.

19

- Add cheese sauce and butter into the pot, and cook until you see that butter has melted and everything is thoroughly combined.
- Sprinkle some salt and pepper according to your taste.
- Add cheese sauce, shredded cheddar cheese, pasta- cheese mixture and remaining cheese sauce respectively over the pizza crust in the baking dish.
- Bake this in the preheated oven for about 10 minutes.
- Let it stand as it is for about 2 minutes before slicing it into pieces.

Serving: 4

Timing Information:

Preparation	Cooking	Total Time
10 mins	25 mins	35 mins

Nutritional Information:

Calories	584 kcal
Carbohydrates	64.6 g
Cholesterol	59 mg
Fat	26 g
Fiber	2.5 g
Protein	25.9 g
Sodium	1186 mg

* Percent Daily Values are based on a 2,000 calorie diet.

MAC & CHEESE POBLANO

Ingredients

- 1 tbsps butter
- 1 medium onion, chopped
- 1/2 cup red bell pepper, chopped
- 1 cup medium tomato, chopped
- 1 clove garlic, chopped
- 1/8 tsp salt
- 1/8 tsp ground black pepper
- 1 (10.75 ounce) can Campbell's® Condensed Creamy Poblano & Queso Soup
- 3/4 cup milk
- 1 cup shredded Cheddar cheese
- 8 ounces elbow macaroni, cooked and drained
- 2 tbsps chopped cilantro

Directions

- Cook onion and pepper in hot butter for about 5 minutes before adding tomato and garlic, and cooking all this for another 1 minute.

- Sprinkle some salt and pepper according to your taste before stirring in soup and milk, and bringing all this to boil.
- Add cheese after turning the heat off and then add macaroni.
- Sprinkle some cilantro before serving.

Serving: 8

Timing Information:

Preparation	Cooking	Total Time
20 mins	10 mins	30 mins

Nutritional Information:

Calories	240 kcal
Carbohydrates	28.6 g
Cholesterol	22 mg
Fat	9.9 g
Fiber	2 g
Protein	9.1 g
Sodium	420 mg

* Percent Daily Values are based on a 2,000 calorie diet.

HENWOOD MAC AND CHEESE

Ingredients

- 1/2 (16 ounce) package fusilli (spiral) pasta
- 1/4 cup margarine
- 1 tbsps minced onion
- 1/4 cup all-purpose flour
- 2 cups milk
- 4 ounces processed cheese food
- 1/4 cup blue cheese crumbles
- 1/4 cup cubed Cheddar cheese
- 1 tsp salt
- 1 pinch ground black pepper
- 1/4 tsp dry mustard

Directions

- Set your oven at 400 degrees F and also put some oil on the baking dish.
- Cook pasta in boiling salty water for about 12 minutes before

draining it with the help of colander.

- Cook onion in hot margarine for about 5 minutes before adding flour and cooking it for another one minute.
- Pour milk into the mixture slowly, while stirring continuously until you see that it is thoroughly combined.
- Now add cheese food, pepper, blue cheese, Cheddar cheese, salt and mustard into the mixture and cook this until you see that cheese has melted.
- Stir in pasta.
- Bake this in the preheated oven for about 20 minutes or until the top begins to turn brown.

Serving: 10

Timing Information:

Preparation	Cooking	Total Time
15 mins	35 mins	50 mins

Nutritional Information:

Calories	375 kcal
Carbohydrates	35.8 g
Cholesterol	34 mg
Fat	19.4 g
Fiber	1.5 g
Protein	15.1 g
Sodium	905 mg

* Percent Daily Values are based on a 2,000 calorie diet.

MATZO MAC AND CHEESE

Ingredients

- 2 cups milk
- 1 1/2 cups sour cream
- 1 (8 ounce) package shredded Cheddar cheese
- 3 eggs
- 3 tbsps butter, melted
- 1 tsp salt
- 1/4 tsp ground black pepper
- 3 cups matzo farfel

Directions

- Set your oven at 400 degrees F and also put some oil on the baking dish.
- Combine all the ingredients mentioned above in a medium sized bowl before pouring it into baking dish.

- Bake this in the preheated oven for about 40 minutes or until the top begins to turn brown.

Serving: 10

Timing Information:

Preparation	Cooking	Total Time
15 mins	30 mins	35 mins

Nutritional Information.

Calories	314 kcal
Carbohydrates	20.1 g
Cholesterol	108 mg
Fat	20.6 g
Fiber	0 g
Protein	12.2 g
Sodium	456 mg

* Percent Daily Values are based on a 2,000 calorie diet.
Nutrition

☐

MAC AND CHEESE SOUP I

Ingredients

- 3 cups elbow macaroni
- 1 (10.75 ounce) can cream of mushroom soup
- 2 cups shredded Cheddar cheese, divided
- 1/2 cup milk
- 1/2 tsp prepared mustard
- 1 pinch ground black pepper
- 1 cup French-fried onions

Directions

- Set your oven at 400 degrees F and also put some oil on the baking dish.
- Cook elbow macaroni in boiling salty water for about 8 minutes before draining it with the help of a colander.

- Coat macaroni with the mixture of mushroom soup, pepper, cheddar cheese, mustard and milk very thoroughly before pouring it into the baking dish.
- Bake this in the preheated oven for about 25 minutes before adding remaining cheddar cheese and fried onion, and baking all this for another five minutes.

Serving: 4

Timing Information:

Preparation	Cooking	Total Time
10 mins	40 mins	50 mins

Nutritional Information:

Calories	961 kcal
Carbohydrates	90.3 g
Cholesterol	62 mg
Fat	53 g
Fiber	2.6 g
Protein	26.6 g
Sodium	1347 mg

* Percent Daily Values are based on a 2,000 calorie diet.
Nutrition

☐

VEGETABLE MAC AND CHEESE

Ingredients

- 1 (12 ounce) box Barilla® Veggie Elbows
- 1/2 cup panko bread crumbs
- 5 tbsps extra-virgin olive oil, divided
- 1 clove garlic
- 5 okra, sliced
- 2 cups heavy cream
- 1 cup shredded fontina cheese
- 1 cup shredded Asiago cheese
- 1/2 cup grated Parmigiano cheese
- salt and white pepper to taste

Directions

- Cook panko bread crumbs in hot olive oil for about three minutes or until brown and crispy.
- Now cook garlic in hot olive oil for a few minutes before adding

okra and cooking it for another one minute.

- Pour heavy cream into it and cook it for a few more minutes.
- Turn off the heat and stir in fontina and asiago cheese.
- Cook paste by following the direction of the package and coat it with sauce and parmigiana cheese.
- Sprinkle salt and pepper according to your taste, and top all this with bread crumbs.
- Serve.

Serving: 4

Timing Information:

Preparation	Cooking	Total Time
20 mins	20 mins	40 mins

Nutritional Information:

Calories	1151 kcal
Carbohydrates	77.1 g
Cholesterol	227 mg
Fat	81.9 g
Fiber	5 g
Protein	33.9 g
Sodium	863 mg

* Percent Daily Values are based on a 2,000 calorie diet.

☐

MAGGIE'S FAVORITE MAC AND CHEESE

Ingredients

- 1 3/4 cups elbow macaroni, uncooked
- 3 tbsps butter or margarine
- 2 tbsps flour
- 2 cups milk
- 2 cups KRAFT Shredded Sharp Cheddar Cheese, divided
- 3 slices OSCAR MAYER Center Cut Bacon, cooked, crumbled

Directions

- Set your oven at 350 degrees F and also put some oil on the baking dish.
- Cook pasta in boiling salty water for about 8 minutes before draining it with the help of a colander.

- Cook flour in hot butter before adding milk, while stirring continuously for 5 minutes.
- Now add cheese before cooking all this for another 5 minutes or until you see that the sauce is thick enough.
- Add this sauce over macaroni and bacon before pouring this into the prepared dish.
- Bake this in the preheated oven for about 30 minutes or until the top begins to turn brown.

Serving: 6

Timing Information:

Preparation	Cooking	Total Time
20 mins	20 mins	40 mins

Nutritional Information:

Calories	385 kcal
Carbohydrates	30 g
Cholesterol	60 mg
Fat	21.8 g
Fiber	1.1 g
Protein	16.5 g
Sodium	411 mg

* Percent Daily Values are based on a 2,000 calorie diet.
Nutrition

CLASSIC MAC AND CHEESE I

Ingredients

- 2 cups macaroni
- 1/2 cup nonfat cottage cheese
- 1 egg white
- 1/2 packet artificial sweetener
- 1/4 cup reduced fat processed cheese food, cubed
- 1/4 cup lowfat buttermilk
- 1/4 tsp liquid smoke flavoring
- 1/2 cup crushed saltine crackers

Directions

- Set your oven at 400 degrees F and also put some oil on the baking dish.
- Cook pasta in boiling salty water for about 8 minutes before draining it with the help of a colander.

- Mix blended cottage cheese, cheese food, egg white, sweetener, buttermilk and liquid smoke in medium sized bowl before pouring this into prepared dish.
- Top all this with crushed crackers.
- Bake this in the preheated oven for about 30 minutes or until the top begins to turn brown.

Serving: 4

Timing Information:

Preparation	Cooking	Total Time
5 mins	38 mins	43 mins

Nutritional Information:

Calories	291 kcal
Carbohydrates	48.9 g
Cholesterol	6 mg
Fat	3.4 g
Fiber	1.9 g
Protein	14.9 g
Sodium	412 mg

* Percent Daily Values are based on a 2,000 calorie diet.

☐

BUFFALO CHICKEN MAC AND CHEESE

Ingredients

- cooking spray
- 1 (16 ounce) package elbow macaroni
- 1 (16 ounce) container sour cream
- 1 (8 ounce) package cream cheese, softened
- 1 (12 fluid ounce) can evaporated milk
- 1 (12 fluid ounce) bottle Buffalo wing sauce (such as Frank's®)
- 1 (1 ounce) package ranch dressing mix
- 1 rotisserie chicken, meat removed and chopped
- 2 cups shredded Cheddar cheese, divided
- 1 cup panko bread crumbs
- 1/4 cup melted butter

Directions

- Set your oven at 350 degrees F and also put some oil on the baking dish.
- Cook elbow macaroni in boiling salty water for about 8 minutes before draining it with the help of a colander.
- Add evaporated milk, buffalo wing sauce and ranch dressing into the mixture of sour cream and cream cheese before adding shredded chicken, cheddar cheese and macaroni.
- Top macaroni mixture in the baking dish with bread crumbs and remaining cheddar cheese before adding some butter over all this.
- Bake this in the preheated oven for about 30 minutes or until the top begins to turn brown.

Serving: 8

Timing Information:

Preparation	Cooking	Total Time
15 mins	30 mins	45 mins

Nutritional Information:

Calories	917 kcal
Carbohydrates	67.1 g
Cholesterol	180 mg
Fat	53.3 g
Fiber	1.8 g
Protein	44.7 g
Sodium	1730 mg

* Percent Daily Values are based on a 2,000 calorie diet.
☐

HEALTH CONSCIENCE MAC AND CHEESE

Ingredients

- 1 (16 ounce) package whole wheat macaroni (such as Smart Taste ®)
- 2 tbsps butter
- 2 1/2 tbsps all-purpose flour
- 2 cups shredded low-fat Cheddar cheese
- 1/2 cup grated Parmesan cheese
- 3 cups low-fat (1%) milk
- 2 tbsps butter
- 1/2 cup whole wheat bread crumbs
- 1 pinch paprika

Directions

- Set your oven at 400 degrees F and also put some oil on the baking dish.

- Cook elbow macaroni in boiling salty water for about 8 minutes before draining it with the help of a colander.
- Cook flour in hot butter before adding milk, while stirring continuously.
- Now add cheddar and parmesan cheese before cooking all this for another 3 minutes or until you see that the sauce is thick enough.
- Pour this sauce over macaroni in a baking dish.
- Cook bread crumbs in hot butter until crispy and put this and paprika over macaroni in the baking dish.
- Bake this in the preheated oven for about 30 minutes or until the top begins to turn brown.

Serving: 4

Timing Information:

Preparation	Cooking	Total Time
20 mins	30 mins	50 mins

Nutritional Information:

Calories	770 kcal
Carbohydrates	106.6 g
Cholesterol	60 mg
Fat	22.4 g
Fiber	10.6 g
Protein	42.5 g
Sodium	750 mg

* Percent Daily Values are based on a 2,000 calorie diet.

MAC AND CHEESE SOUP II

(SPICY VERSION)

Ingredients

- 2 (7.25 ounce) packages macaroni and cheese mix
- 1/4 cup butter
- 2 cups chicken broth
- 1 (14.5 ounce) can diced tomatoes with green chili peppers
- 1 tbsps garlic powder
- 1 tsp ground cumin
- 1 tsp dry mustard powder
- 1/2 tsp ground black pepper, or to taste
- 1 1/2 cups milk
- 3/4 cup sour cream, divided

Directions

- Cook elbow macaroni in boiling salty water for about 8 minutes before draining it with the help of a colander.

- Cook the mixture of cooked macaroni, butter, tomatoes and chicken broth over medium heat before adding garlic, all the content of cheese mix packets, cumin, pepper, milk and dry mustard, and cook all this at low heat.
- Top each bowl that you serve with 2 tbsps of sour cream.

Serving: 6

Timing Information:

Preparation	Cooking	Total Time
10 mins	20 mins	30 mins

Nutritional Information:

Calories	434 kcal
Carbohydrates	54.2 g
Cholesterol	49 mg
Fat	17.9 g
Fiber	2.3 g
Protein	15.2 g
Sodium	1230 mg

* Percent Daily Values are based on a 2,000 calorie diet.
□

MAC AND CHEESE SOUP III

(BACON, ONION)

Ingredients

- 3 slices bacon, chopped(optional)
- 1 tsp bacon drippings
- 1 (7 ounce) package elbow macaroni
- 1 small onion, finely chopped
- 1/4 tsp minced garlic, or to taste
- 2 (14 ounce) cans chicken broth
- 1 (16 ounce) jar cheese sauce (such as Ragu® Double Cheddar)
- 2 tbsps chicken bouillon granules
- 2 tsps ground red chili pepper, or to taste
- 1 tsp ground black pepper
- 1 pinch crushed red pepper flakes, or to taste

Directions

- Cook chopped bacon in a large skillet for about seven minutes before draining it with the help of a paper towel-lined plate.
- Cook pasta in boiling salty water for about 8 minutes before draining it with the help of a colander.
- Now cook onion in bacon drippings for about 5 minutes over medium heat before adding garlic and cooking it for 2 more minutes.
- Stir in bacon bits, ground red chili pepper, chicken broth, cheese sauce, crushed red pepper flakes, chicken bouillon granules, black pepper and cooked macaroni, and bring all this to boil before turning down the heat to and cooking it for another 5 minute.
- Serve.

Serving: 6

Timing Information:

Preparation	Cooking	Total Time
15 mins	30 mins	45 mins

Nutritional Information:

Calories	341 kcal
Carbohydrates	34.1 g
Cholesterol	36 mg
Fat	16.2 g
Fiber	1.7 g
Protein	14.3 g
Sodium	1509 mg

* Percent Daily Values are based on a 2,000 calorie diet.

☐

SLOW COOKER MAC AND CHEESE

Ingredients

- 1 (16 ounce) package elbow macaroni
- 1/2 cup butter
- salt and ground black pepper to taste
- 1 (16 ounce) package shredded Cheddar cheese, divided
- 1 (5 ounce) can evaporated milk
- 2 eggs, well beaten
- 2 cups whole milk
- 1 (10.75 ounce) can condensed Cheddar cheese soup (such as Campbell's®)
- 1 pinch paprika, or as desired(optional)

Directions

- Cook macaroni in boiling salty water for about 8 minutes before draining it with the help of a colander.
- Add butter, salt, pepper and half cheddar cheese into the pasta, while mixing it thoroughly.
- Pour the mixture of evaporated milk and eggs into the pasta mixture before adding the mixture of milk and cheddar cheese soup.
- Add the remaining cheese over this mixture and garnish with paprika.
- Cook this on low heat for three hour before serving.

Serving: 12

Timing Information:

Preparation	Cooking	Total Time
15 mins	3 hr 10 mins	3 hr 25 mins

Nutritional Information:

Calories	432 kcal
Carbohydrates	33.9 g
Cholesterol	99 mg
Fat	24.7 g
Fiber	1.4 g
Protein	17.8 g
Sodium	524 mg

* Percent Daily Values are based on a 2,000 calorie diet.
□

AMERICAN MAC AND CHEESE

Ingredients

- 2 pounds uncooked elbow macaroni
- 2 (10.75 ounce) cans condensed Cheddar cheese soup
- 4 eggs, beaten
- 2 3/4 cups milk
- 2 pounds Cheddar cheese, shredded, divided
- salt and pepper to taste

Directions

- Set your oven at 400 degrees F and also put some oil on the baking dish.
- Cook macaroni in boiling salty water for about 8 minutes before draining it with the help of a colander.

- Pour the mixture of cooked macaroni, cheese, milk, salt, eggs, pepper and soup into the baking dish.
- Top all this with the remaining cheese.
- Bake this in the preheated oven for about 45 minutes covered and 15 minutes uncovered or until the top begins to turn brown.

Serving: 16

Timing Information:

Preparation	Cooking	Total Time
10 mins	1 hr 10 mins	1 hr 20 mins

Nutritional Information:

Calories	537 kcal
Carbohydrates	49.6 g
Cholesterol	118 mg
Fat	25.3 g
Fiber	2.9 g
Protein	26.9 g
Sodium	669 mg

* Percent Daily Values are based on a 2,000 calorie diet.
Nutrition

☐

CHICKEN AND SAUSAGE MAC AND CHEESE

Ingredients

- 1 cup uncooked macaroni
- 1 link of precooked chicken and cheese sausage
- 1 tbsps milk
- 1 tsp butter
- 1 tbsps grated Parmesan cheese
- 1/4 cup shredded mozzarella cheese

Directions

- Cook pasta in boiling salty water for about 8 minutes before draining it with the help of a colander.
- Heat up sliced sausage in microwave for about 30 seconds before mixing it thoroughly with macaroni, mozzarella cheese,

milk, parmesan cheese and
butter.
- Serve.

Serving: 2

Timing Information:

Preparation	Cooking	Total Time
10 mins	10 mins	20 mins

Nutritional Information:

Calories	354 kcal
Carbohydrates	42.1 g
Cholesterol	53 mg
Fat	11 g
Fiber	1.7 g
Protein	19.6 g
Sodium	651 mg

* Percent Daily Values are based on a 2,000 calorie diet.
Nutrition

26%

☐

TUNA MAC AND CHEESE

Ingredients

- 1 cup uncooked egg noodles
- 2 1/2 cups sharp Cheddar cheese, shredded
- 1/4 cup milk
- 1/4 cup butter
- 1/3 cup cottage cheese
- 2 tbsps sour cream
- 1 (12 ounce) can tuna, drained
- 1 1/2 cups green peas

Directions

- Cook elbow macaroni in boiling salty water for about 8 minutes before draining it with the help of a colander.
- Mix cheddar cheese, sour cream, milk, cottage cheese and butter over medium heat until melted.

- Add cooked noodles into the cheese mixture before stirring in canned tuna and green peas.
- Heat thoroughly before serving.

Serving: 5

Timing Information:

Preparation	Cooking	Total Time
5 mins	20 mins	25 mins

Nutritional Information:

Calories	535 kcal
Carbohydrates	13.7 g
Cholesterol	129 mg
Fat	35.2 g
Fiber	2.2 g
Protein	40.3 g
Sodium	648 mg

* Percent Daily Values are based on a 2,000 calorie diet.
Nutrition

MAC AND CHEESE SOUP IV

(BROCCOLI, ONION, HAM)

Ingredients

- 1 (14 ounce) package uncooked macaroni and cheese
- 1 cup chopped broccoli
- 1/2 cup chopped onion
- 1 cup water
- 2 1/2 cups milk
- 1 (11 ounce) can condensed cream of Cheddar cheese soup
- 1 cup cubed cooked ham

Directions

- Cook elbow macaroni in boiling salty water for about 8 minutes before draining it with the help of a colander.
- Bring the mixture of broccoli, water and onion to boil, and cook

until you see that broccoli is
tender.

- Now add macaroni, ham, cheese
  mixture, soup and milk into it
  before bringing all this to boil
  again.
- Serve.

Serving: 6

Timing Information:

Preparation	Cooking	Total Time
15 mins	15 mins	30 mins

Nutritional Information:

Calories	422 kcal
Carbohydrates	55.7 g
Cholesterol	42 mg
Fat	12.9 g
Fiber	2.4 g
Protein	20.9 g
Sodium	1248 mg

* Percent Daily Values are based on a 2,000 calorie diet.

GUADALAJARA MAC AND CHEESE

(MEXICAN MAC AND CHEESE II)

Ingredients

- 1 1/2 pounds lean ground beef
- 2 tbsps dried onion flakes
- 2 (7.25 ounce) packages dry macaroni and cheese
- 15 ounces nacho cheese dip
- 1 cup medium salsa
- 1 (7 ounce) can diced green chilis

Directions

- Cook beef and onion over high heat until you see that beef is brown.
- Now cook macaroni and cheese by following the directions of the package before adding meat and onion mixture, green chilis,

nacho cheese dip and salsa, and cooking all this at low heat for about 15 minutes.

* Serve.

Serving: 8

Timing Information:

Preparation	Cooking	Total Time
20 mins	40 mins	1 hr

Nutritional Information:

Calories	454 kcal
Carbohydrates	44.4 g
Cholesterol	71 mg
Fat	18.2 g
Fiber	2.8 g
Protein	26.4 g
Sodium	1398 mg

* Percent Daily Values are based on a 2,000 calorie diet.

A GIFT FROM ME TO YOU...

<u>Send the Book!</u>

I know you like easy cooking. But what about Japanese Sushi?

Join my private reader's club and get a copy of *Infinite Sushi: A Complete Set of Sushi and Japanese Recipes* by fellow BookSumo author Hashimoto Kazuma for FREE!

Send the Book!

Enjoy some of the best sushi available!

You will also receive updates about all my new books when they are free. So please show your support.

Also don't forget to like and subscribe on the social networks. I love meeting my readers. Links to all my profiles are below so please click and connect :)

Facebook

Twitter

COME ON...
LET'S BE FRIENDS :)

I adore my readers and love connecting with them socially. Please follow the links below so we can connect on Facebook, Twitter, and Google+.

Facebook

Twitter

I also have a blog that I regularly update for my readers so check it out below.

My Blog

CAN I ASK A FAVOUR?

If you found this book interesting, or have otherwise found any benefit in it. Then may I ask that you post a review of it on Amazon? Nothing excites me more than new reviews, especially reviews which suggest new topics for writing. I do read all reviews and I always factor feedback into my newer works.

So if you are willing to take ten minutes to write what you sincerely thought about this book then please visit our Amazon page and post your opinions.

Again thank you!

INTERESTED IN OTHER EASY COOKBOOKS?

Everything is easy! Check out my Amazon Author page for more great cookbooks:

For a complete listing of all my books please see my author page at:

http://amazon.com/author/maggiechow